SAVE OUR EARTH!
Climate Action Explained

HELPING THE OCEAN

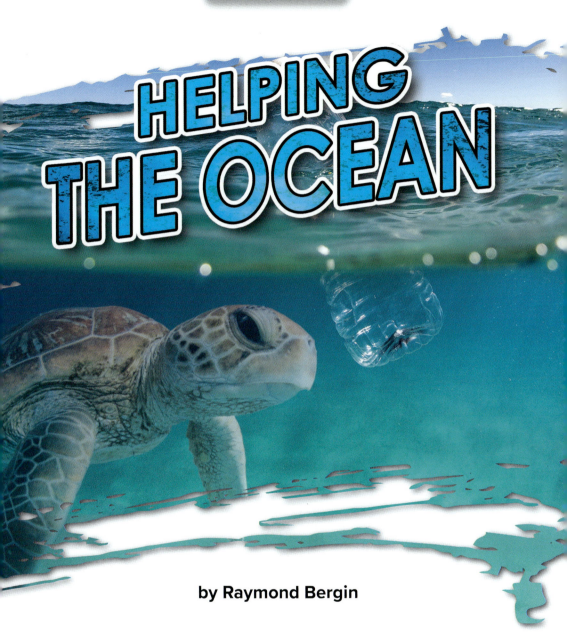

by Raymond Bergin

Minneapolis, Minnesota

Credits
Cover and title page, © Philip Thurston/iStock; 4–5, © Ibrahim Chalhoub/Getty Images; 6BR, © Mainlander NZ/Shutterstock; 8–9, © Nature Picture Library/Alamy Stock Photo 10–11, © David Salvatori/VWPics/ Alamy Stock Photo; 12–13, © photography by p. lubas/Getty Images; 14, © ullstein bild/Getty Images; 15, © Cindy Hopkins/Alamy Stock Photo; 16–17, © PA Images/Alamy Stock Photo; 18BR, © Andrew b Stowe/ Shutterstock; 19, © SeaForester; 19TR, © SeaForester; 20–21, © Roy Perring/Alamy Stock Photo; 22–23, © Martijn Alderse Baas/Shutterstock; 25, © PA Images/ Alamy Stock Photo 26–27, © ljubaphoto/iStock; 28, © Rainer von Brandis/iStock; 29TL, © PeopleImages/iStock; 29UML, © FG Trade Latin/iStock; 29ML, © doble–d/iStock; 29BML, © damircudic/iStock; 29BL, © gradyreese/iStock

Bearport Publishing Company Product Development Team
Publisher: Jen Jenson; Director of Product Development: Spencer Brinker; Managing Editor: Allison Juda; Editor: Cole Nelson; Associate Editor: Tiana Tran; Production Editor: Naomi Reich; Designer: Kim Jones; Designer: Kayla Eggert; Designer: Steve Scheluchin; Production Specialist: Owen Hamlin

Statement on Usage of Generative Artificial Intelligence
Bearport Publishing remains committed to publishing high-quality nonfiction books. Therefore, we restrict the use of generative AI to ensure accuracy of all text and visual components pertaining to a book's subject. See BearportPublishing.com for details.

Library of Congress Cataloging-in-Publication Data is available at www.loc.gov or upon request from the publisher.

ISBN: 979-8-89577-053-5 (hardcover)
ISBN: 979-8-89577-170-9 (ebook)

Copyright © 2026 Bearport Publishing Company. All rights reserved. No part of this publication may be reproduced in whole or in part, stored in any retrieval system, or transmitted in any form or by any means, electronic, mechanical, photocopying, recording, or otherwise, without written permission from the publisher. Bearport Publishing is a division of FlutterBee Education Group.

For more information, write to Bearport Publishing, 3500 American Blvd W, Suite 150, Bloomington, MN 55431.

Contents

Commotion in the Ocean 4

Our Blue Planet Heats Up 6

Shell Shock 8

What a Dump! 10

Disappearing Fish 12

Protecting the Ocean: Pristine Seas 14

Restoring Reefs: Coral Vita 16

Helping Kelp: SeaForester 18

Copying Nature: Living Seawalls 20

Collecting Pollution: Great Bubble Barrier . . 22

An App for That: Abalobi 24

Taking Action for Tomorrow 26

Save the Ocean! 28

Glossary 30

Read More 31

Learn More Online 31

Index 32

About the Author 32

Commotion in the Ocean

Waves lap along the seashore where a fleet of fishing boats makes their way out of the harbor. They cruise through the water, which is warmer and crashes farther inland than it did decades ago. Many of the shorebirds that once swooped through the sky above the beach are gone. They left as the fish and crabs below began to disappear. Plastic floats past a new hotel, restaurant, and boardwalk—all built where a **kelp** forest used to support many fish. What on Earth is going on with the ocean, and how can we fix it?

The ocean has the most livable space of any habitat on the planet. Scientists estimate that between 50 and 80 percent of all life on Earth can be found in the ocean.

The ocean contains almost 97 percent of Earth's liquid water.

Our Blue Planet Heats Up

Earth's ocean is brimming with hundreds of thousands of known **species** of plants and animals, but this vast watery home is threatened by human actions. We burn **fossil fuels** to power our cars, factories, and homes. As we do, we release a lot of gases—including **carbon dioxide**—into the **atmosphere**. Many of these gases trap heat around the planet.

Global air and water temperatures are on the rise because of these heat-trapping gases. Many plant and animal species cannot survive in the warming waters.

As water warms, it expands. This leads to coastal flooding. The lives of plants, animals, and even humans living along the shore are put in danger by rising sea levels.

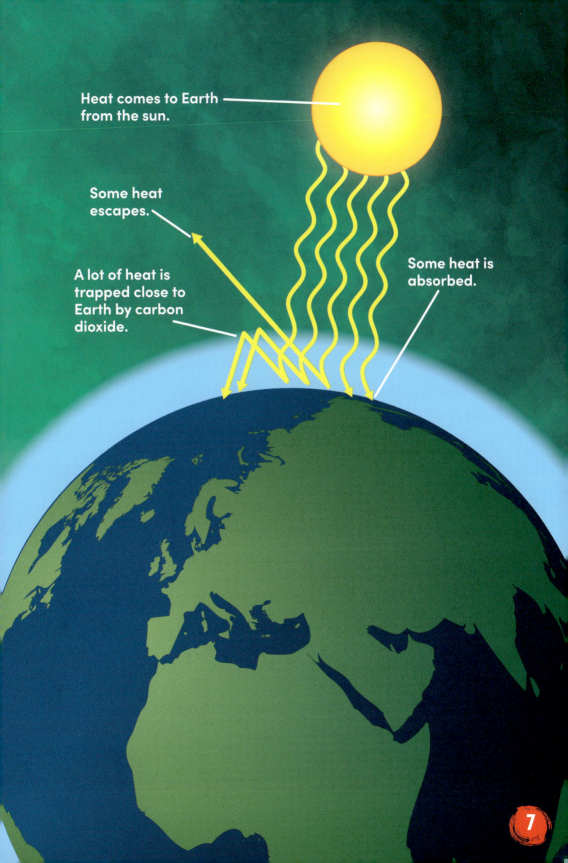

Shell Shock

About a third of the carbon dioxide released by burning fossil fuels is absorbed into the ocean. This is making the water more acidic. It can harm the ability of some **invertebrates**, such as oysters, clams, and corals, to build their shells and protective structures. The hard coverings may even start to fall apart in extremely acidic waters. These waters can also harm fish. Clown fish, for example, can have trouble sensing predators as well as finding food and shelter when the water gets very acidic.

Coral reefs support about 25 percent of marine plants and animals at some point during their lives. But some scientists believe increasingly acidic water and rising temperatures may cause reefs to disappear by 2100.

What a Dump!

Carbon dioxide is not the only thing polluting Earth's waters. Every year, about 40 billion pounds (18 billion kg) of plastic waste ends up in the ocean. Some sea creatures get tangled in the plastic. Others mistake it for food and get sick from eating the trash.

To make matters worse, once plastic is in the water, it does not go away. Plastic food containers, water bottles, and shopping bags may be used on land for only a few minutes. But once in the ocean, they stay there for centuries.

As plastic slowly breaks down, it releases harmful chemicals. As many as 2,400 chemicals from plastics can poison sea creatures.

Disappearing Fish

Life in the ocean faces an even more direct threat—overfishing. Because of large industrial fishing operations, sea creatures are being pulled from the ocean faster than they can reproduce. As a result, the number of fish in the sea is plummeting.

Around the world, fishing ships catch about 100 million tons (91 million t) of fish every year. In many parts of the ocean, fish populations have **collapsed**. About one-third of the world's fishing grounds are considered overfished.

About 38 million people have jobs in the **marine** fishing industry. The collapse of Canada's Grand Banks fishery in 1992 left 35,000 fishers without jobs.

Protecting the Ocean
Pristine Seas

While Earth's ocean faces difficult challenges, there are many people taking action against the threats. Pristine Seas is a project working to use exploration, research, and storytelling to encourage people to protect our watery world.

Currently, only 3 percent of the ocean is highly protected. In these areas, fishing and construction are banned while marine life is allowed to recover. Pristine Seas hopes to increase that number to 30 percent of the world's marine areas by 2030. The project works with **Indigenous** peoples, local communities, and governments. Together, they find ways to protect and restore the ocean.

Pristine Seas helped Costa Rica's Cocos Island National Park grow 27 times larger. A fishing ban there now protects the area's **endangered** sharks and sea turtles.

Pristine Seas has established 28 marine reserves worldwide with a total area equal to twice the size of India.

Restoring Reefs
Coral Vita

Half of Earth's coral reefs have disappeared in the last 70 years, but Coral Vita is working to change that. This company grows corals on reef structures in land-based farms until they are **mature**. They then plant the structures within weakened reefs in the ocean, helping restore the sick reefs to health.

By increasing the water temperature and acidity in the grow tanks, Coral Vita is also able to raise coral that is more **resilient**. The company's method trains the farmed coral to better survive the effects of climate change.

Coral Vita has planted more than 15,000 land-grown corals in the Bahamas, where the company is based. In some areas with the new corals, fish populations have doubled.

Coral Vita is able to grow healthy coral in tanks on land up to 50 times faster than coral growing in the ocean.

Helping Kelp
SeaForester

Kelp is a strong ally in the fight against climate change. Like other plants, kelp absorbs heat-trapping carbon dioxide and turns it into **oxygen**. But warming waters, coastal **development**, and pollution have caused half of all kelp forests to disappear over the last 50 years.

SeaForester is working to reverse the loss of kelp forests. The company covers stones with kelp **spores** and scatters them in the ocean. The spores **germinate** in reefs on the ocean floor and grow into new kelp forests. SeaForester aims to plant thousands of tons of kelp forests by 2026.

Kelps remove more carbon from the air than land-based plants. They absorb 5 million tn. (4.5 million t) of carbon annually. This is equivalent to the yearly **emissions** of about one million gasoline-powered cars.

Stones covered with kelp spores

A SeaForester worker throws stones covered in kelp spores into the ocean to help healthy kelp forests.

Copying Nature
Living Seawalls

Many kelp and seaweed forests have been uprooted to make room for human-made seawalls that protect coastal development from pounding waves and floodwaters. The thousands of species of marine life that rely upon these forests disappear along with the greenery.

To address this concern, Living Seawalls builds barriers made of panels with surfaces that are similar to those of natural structures. The seawalls protect human communities from rising seawater, while also providing nooks and crannies for communities of seaweeds, fish, and other marine life.

Living Seawalls panels increase the number of marine species in an area by up to 36 percent. One installation in Australia attracted 115 species—about the same as can be found on natural rocky reefs.

Living Seawalls have textured surfaces that promote marine life.

Collecting Pollution
Great Bubble Barrier

Much of the plastic that ends up in our ocean is carried there by trash-littered rivers. To help fix this problem, some inventors have come up with a surprising idea—using bubbles. The Great Bubble Barrier stops river trash before it reaches the ocean. The system uses a series of underwater tubes to pump air into rivers to create a curtain of bubbles. Each of these bubble barriers pushes plastic trash to the water's surface. Once there, it can be collected. The Great Bubble Barrier systems can catch about 86 percent of the plastic waste from the rivers and canals where they have been installed.

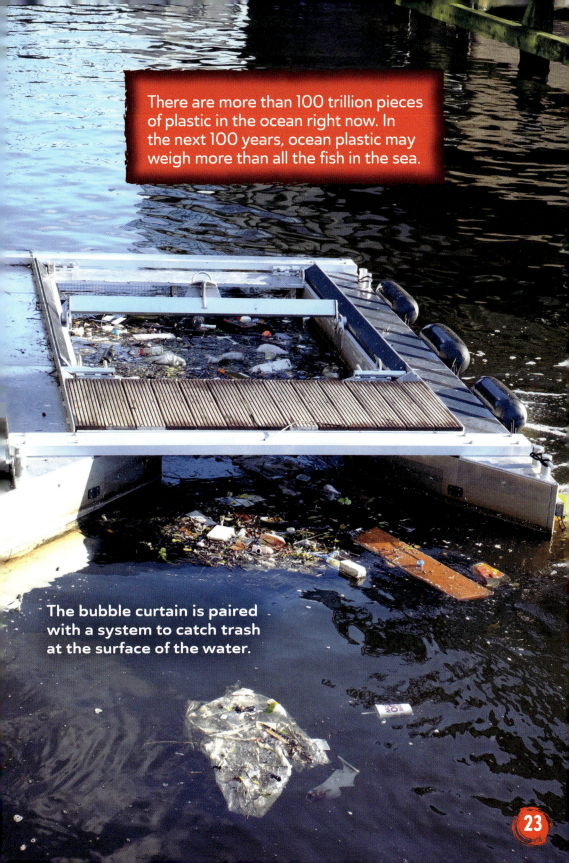

There are more than 100 trillion pieces of plastic in the ocean right now. In the next 100 years, ocean plastic may weigh more than all the fish in the sea.

The bubble curtain is paired with a system to catch trash at the surface of the water.

An App for That
Abalobi

To fight overfishing, an organization called Abalobi is turning to tech. They developed three connected apps that help track fish populations while also supporting fishing communities. The Fishers app allows fishers to send daily catch information to a database. Then, the Marketplace app shows restaurants and food shoppers which fish are available. Scientists use the Monitor app to study the fishers' daily catch data to identify stressed fish populations and overfished areas. Together, the three apps support all aspects of the market to encourage fishing practices that are better for the planet.

More than 6,000 fishers from 12 countries use the Abalobi apps. Where 60 percent of their catches were once taken from threatened fish species, now 90 percent are from sustainable and rebounding fish populations.

Abalobi fishers collect information about their catches.

Taking Action for Tomorrow

The problems facing Earth's ocean can seem overwhelming. Human-created threats are killing marine life, flooding coastlines, and endangering the overall health of the planet. But all around the world, people are working hard to help.

The watery world provides shelter and food to millions of species. It's a crucial part of the human food supply. We have no choice but to take action to protect and preserve the ocean for today and into the future. Together, we can save our Earth!

Currently, about 44 percent of the global population lives within 100 miles (160 km) of a coastline. What happens to the water can directly impact these global citizens.

Save the Ocean!

Saving the ocean and the life it contains seems like a huge job. But there are small, everyday steps we can take to keep the sea and coastlines clean. These small steps build to shift efforts in the right direction.

Avoid single-use plastic items. Instead, carry your own reusable shopping bags, water bottles, and food containers.

Always place your trash into secure garbage containers or recycling bins when boating or doing things near the shore.

Take part in beach cleanup days and coastal habitat restoration projects.

Write to your political representatives to urge them to support pro-environment policies.

If it is possible and safe, walk, ride a bike, or take public transportation instead of releasing carbon dioxide into the air by taking a personal car.

Glossary

atmosphere the layer of gases that surrounds Earth

carbon dioxide an invisible gas in the air that is released when fossil fuels are burned

collapsed broken down completely

development the use of land for human activity, commonly including building new construction

emissions substances, such as gases and soot, released into the air by fuel-burning engines

endangered at risk of becoming extinct in the near future

fossil fuels sources of energy made from the remains of animals and plants that lived long ago

germinate to cause to sprout or begin to grow

Indigenous originating from a particular place; often a term used for the first people in an area

invertebrates animals that don't have backbones or any other bones

kelp a type of seaweed that grows in long green or brown strips

marine having to do with the ocean

mature fully grown or developed

oxygen a colorless gas found in air and water that people and other animals need to breathe

resilient capable of withstanding shock or change

species groups that animals are divided into, according to similar characteristics

spores tiny structures that are able to become new individuals of that life form

Read More

Bergin, Raymond. *Ocean Life Connections (Life on Earth! Biodiversity Explained).* Minneapolis: Bearport Publishing Company, 2023.

Knutson, Julie. *Do the Work! Climate Action, Life Below Water, and Life on Land (Committing to the UN's Sustainable Development Goals).* Ann Arbor, MI: Cherry Lake Publishing, 2022.

Sima, Andrew. *Climate: Our Changing World (Science in Action).* Chicago: Albert Whitman & Company, 2023.

Learn More Online

1. Go to **FactSurfer.com** or scan the QR code below.
2. Enter "**Helping the Ocean**" into the search box.
3. Click on the cover of this book to see a list of websites.

Index

acidic water 8

apps 24

birds 4

carbon dioxide 6–8, 10, 18–19, 29

coral 8, 16–17

development 18, 20, 24

fish 4, 8, 12–14, 16, 21, 23–24

fossil fuels 6, 8

invertebrates 8

kelp 4, 18–20

overfishing 12–13, 24

oxygen 18

plastic 4, 10, 22–23, 29

pollution 10, 18, 22

protected areas 14

sea turtles 14

seawalls 20–21

spores 18

trash 10, 22–23, 29

About the Author

Raymond Bergin is a writer who lives in New Jersey and Massachusetts. He loves swimming in the ocean along both of those coastlines.